ANIMALS AT WORK

Animals
Finding Food

WORLD BOOK

World Book, Inc.
180 North LaSalle Street
Suite 900
Chicago, Illinois 60601
USA

Produced for World Book, Inc. by Bailey Publishing Associates Ltd.

For information about other World Book publications, visit our website at **www.worldbook.com** or call **1-800-WORLDBK (967-5325).**

Library of Congress Cataloging-in-Publication data has been applied for.

Title: Animals Finding Food
ISBN: 978-0-7166-2730-2

Animals at Work
ISBN: 978-0-7166-2724-1 (set, hc)

Also available as:
ISBN: 978-0-7166-2743-2 (e-book)

Printed in China by Shenzhen Wing King Tong
Paper Products Co, Ltd., Shenzhen, Guangdong
1st printing August 2018

4346

Staff

Writer: Sean Connolly

Executive Committee

President
Jim O'Rourke

Vice President and Editor in Chief
Paul A. Kobasa

Vice President, Finance
Donald D. Keller

Vice President, Marketing
Jean Lin

Vice President, International
Maksim Rutenberg

Vice President, Technology
Jason Dole

Director, Human Resources
Bev Ecker

Editorial

Director, Print Publishing
Tom Evans

Managing Editor
Jeff De La Rosa

Editor
William D. Adams

Manager, Contracts & Compliance
(Rights & Permissions)
Loranne K. Shields

Manager, Indexing Services
David Pofelski

Librarian
S. Thomas Richardson

Digital

Director, Digital Product
Development
Erika Meller

Digital Product Manager
Jonathan Wills

Manufacturing/Production

Manufacturing Manager
Anne Fritzinger

Proofreader
Nathalie Strassheim

Graphics and Design

Senior Art Director
Tom Evans

Senior Designer
Don Di Sante

Media Editor
Rosalia Bledsoe

Special thanks to:

Roberta Bailey
Nicola Barber
Francis Paola Lea
Claire Munday
Alex Woolf

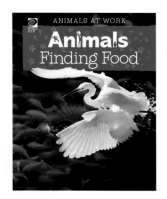

A little egret takes flight over a shoal of goldfish in eastern Asia. Egrets and herons spear fish with their sharp beaks.

Acknowledgments

Cover photo: © Ocean Fishing/Shutterstock

Alamy: 5 (Octavio Campos Salles), 6-7 (Design Pics Inc), 20-21 (Richard Becker), 24-25 (Bob Gibbons), 25 (Science Photo Library), 29 (Nature Picture Library), 30 (Minden Pictures), 32-33 (Cultura Creative), 42-43 (Toby Houlton), 43 (Zute Lightfoot), 45 (Hemis). **National Oceanic and Atmospheric Administration**: 19. **Shutterstock**: title page and 38-39 (Margaret M Stewart), 4 (Hashim Mahrin), 7 (Cathy Withers-Clarke), 8 (Willyam Bradberry), 8-9 (Vladimir Wrangel), 10 (Kesipun), 10-11 (Brian E Kushner), 11 (Cvrestan), 12-13 (Sergey Uryadnikov), 14 (Ariel Celeste Photography), 14-15 (Ondrej Prosicky), 16-17 (MicheleB), 17 (Artsy Imagery), 20 (Abel Tumik), 23 (Utopia_88), 26 (BlueOrange Studio), 26-27 (adrenalinerushdiaries), p27 (Kristina Vackova), 28-29 (Dennis W Donohue), 30-31 (Ed-Ni Photo), 33 (Tom Goaz), 35 (Chase Dekker), 36-37 (Gudkov Andrey), 38 (Nicram Sabod), 39 (Dee Carpenter), 40-41 (Inc), 41 (sirtravelalot), 44 (Apiguide), 44-45 (Natalia Kuzmina).

Contents

Introduction

All living things need energy to survive. Animals grow to large sizes and move very quickly compared to other forms of life, so they need large amounts of energy. They get it by taking in food. This food could be any combination of plants or animals, freshly harvested or long dead. Animals use a wide range of methods to find their food, often doing so in the toughest conditions.

Animals have adapted (changed) over millions of years to be good at collecting their preferred food. The long neck of a giraffe allows it to eat buds and leaves that are too high for other animals to reach. An anteater's long tongue is an excellent tool for reaching deep into ant nests. The streamlined shape of dolphins and falcons lets them swim quickly or dive through the air in pursuit of **prey.**

Animals are often grouped by the type of food that they eat. **Carnivores,** such as tigers, eagles, and sharks, eat meat. Animals that eat only plants are called **herbivores.** They range from the tiniest mice to huge elephants and hippopotamuses. Some animals, including humans, eat both meat and plants. These animals are called **omnivores.**

In this book, you will read about the food animals eat and where they find it. More information on how **predators** catch prey can be found in *Animals Attacking*.

Wide-ranging menu

Omnivores are the most flexible eaters of all animals. When one type of food is scarce—for example, when a forest fire destroys plants—they can eat something else. Omnivores come in all shapes and sizes. The Kodiak bear, a North American bear weighing up to 1,500 pounds (680 kilograms), eats different foods in its Alaskan **habitat,** such as grasses, berries, fish, and even other **mammals.** The pharaoh ant, on the other hand, is only about 0.06 inch (1.5 millimeters) long. Its diet includes **carrion, insects,** nuts, grains, tree sap, and **fungi.**

Pharaoh ants eat their insect prey.

Chasing

Some **predators** chase, catch, and eat other animals. Often, keen senses tell them that **prey** is nearby. They may use speed, agility, or even cooperation with others to hunt down their prey.

HIGH-OCTANE LIFESTYLE

As animals find food and eat, they are taking part in a wider process known as the food web. Energy and **nutrients** pass through this web. Eating food gives an animal energy, but it takes energy to search for it. Animals that rely on speed and agility must hunt more frequently, and they must succeed more often. For instance, the cheetah successfully catches its prey in a little more than half of its chases. If it were less successful, it would run out of energy for its high-speed pursuits and starve.

GROUP STRATEGY

Although most **carnivores** hunt alone, some animals, including wolves, wild dogs, lions, and chimpanzees, hunt in groups. Each animal may have a special thing to do—separating prey mothers from their offspring, guarding against competition from **scavengers,** or making the kill.

Working in groups also allows predators to hunt much larger animals than they could target on their own. North American wolves, for example, may spend days tracking a herd of elk. All the while, they watch for older or weaker members of the herd. The threatening presence of the wolves can cause even larger animals to panic and get caught in underbrush or deep snow—making them easy targets for the pack.

Secretary-birds

Secretary-birds, distant relatives of vultures and hawks, are the only birds of prey that hunt on the ground instead of from the air while flying. They hunt in loose pairs or small groups, catching small **mammals** and **reptiles** in African grasslands. They chase their prey and then strike it with their bill or pound it with their feet. Those feet are adapted to walking rather than grasping, so the bird either eats its catch on the spot or carries it away in its beak. Secretary-birds even hunt and kill **venomous** snakes.

A secretary-bird hunts its prey in the southern African grasslands.

A pack of wolves work together to attack a moose.

UNDERWATER ATTACK

Animals hunt in oceans, streams, and rivers. Many share a streamlined body shape to help them cut through the water. Many have sharp teeth to hold onto struggling **prey.**

Red-bellied piranhas are fish that live in South American lakes and rivers. Their razor-sharp teeth and habit of swimming in **shoals** make them a threat to small **mammals** and other fish. Some people believe piranhas can gang up to take down animals hundreds of times their size. But they only eat much larger animals if they are already dead or dying.

Barracudas patrol temperate (not hot or cold) and tropical ocean waters around the world. They are lone hunters with keen eyesight and sharp teeth. Their long, tubelike bodies help them reach speeds of up to 35 miles (55 kilometers) per hour. These ferocious hunters eat small fish, such as herring, mullet, and anchovies. The streamlined shape that helps them chase down prey also helps them escape from larger **predators,** such as sharks.

The "killing machine"

The great white shark is one of the most frightening hunters in the animal world. Unlike most other sharks, the great white shark is **warm-blooded.** The shark's sharp sense of smell alerts it to potential prey. Then, it swims towards it at up to 35 miles (55 kilometers) per hour. Once the shark has found its prey, it grabs it with its powerful jaws. With 300 teeth in up to seven rows, it does not usually lose its catch once it has attacked.

The great white shark is faster and stronger than other sharks, with a strong sense of smell.

Piranhas have razor-sharp teeth that rip into the flesh of dead or dying prey.

AIRBORNE STRIKE

Bats, birds, and flying **insects** combine speed and agility to dive and swoop in search of **prey.** They use quick reflexes and sharp senses to help them hunt.

The bald eagle mainly eats fish. It spots one swimming near the water's surface and approaches on a low glide above the water. It then snatches the fish from the water with its talons (claws). An eagle can eat about 1 pound (450 grams) of food in four minutes. It holds onto a perch with one foot, grasps the fish with the other, and tears flesh off with its beak.

Other flying **predators** catch their prey in the air. Dragonflies are among the most efficient of all hunters: they successfully catch prey in about 95 percent of their tries. A dragonfly's complex eyes quickly pick out darks spots against the bright sky. Then, the dragonfly uses its powerful wing muscles to fly quickly to its insect prey. Bats also hunt insects, but they use hearing to guide them. They make high-pitched squeaks and pick out moving things by their echoes. This system is called echolocation.

The dragonfly uses its large eyes and powerful wings to hunt its prey.

Air speed record

The peregrine falcon is known as the fastest animal in the world. Although it normally flies at around 45 miles (70 kilometers) per hour, it can reach speeds of up to 200 miles (320 kilometers) per hour in its stoop (hunting dive). With its wings tightly tucked next to its body, the falcon takes on a streamlined shape that cuts through the air like a rocket. It slams into medium-sized birds, such as pigeons and songbirds, stunning or killing them with the force of the impact. At such speeds, air rushing in from the nostrils could harm a bird's lungs. To prevent this, parts of a peregrine's beak guide the airflow away from its nostrils.

A peregrine falcon prepares to go into a stoop.

A bald eagle grabs a fish as it swoops over the water.

Ambushing

Some **predators** wait patiently, often blending in with their surroundings, until another animal gets close enough for them to attack quickly.

PATIENCE IS A VIRTUE

Compared to running, swimming, or flying long distances, lying in wait for **prey** has several advantages. Patient waiting does not use much energy, so ambush predators do not need to eat as often to survive. Also, hiding from prey helps the animal stay hidden from its predators.

Surprise is an important weapon. The Nile crocodile, which lives in Africa, can grow up to 16 feet (4.8 meters) long and weigh 500 pounds (225 kilograms). But it is almost invisible when it is lying in wait in still water, with just the top of its head above the surface. If a wildebeest or buffalo gets close, the crocodile bursts out and grabs its prey in its powerful jaws. It then drags its struggling victim into the water and drowns it.

Animals as different as sea anemones (*uh NEHM uh neez)* and tigers use variations of this same method. The sea anemone, a relative of coral and jellyfish, spends most of its time attached to rocks, waiting for fish to become snared in its **venomous** tentacles. A tiger moves slowly and quietly, waiting to use its size and power to overcome its prey.

DEADLY SQUEEZES

Constricting snakes, such as boas, pythons, and anacondas, do not need **venom** to catch their prey. A constrictor lies in wait until a prey animal passes close by. Then, it grabs hold with its strong jaws and wraps its muscular body around the struggling victim. The prey animal quickly dies, and the snake eats it whole. For years, people believed that the victim died because it could not breathe. New research suggests that a constricting snake kills its prey by cutting off the movement of its blood.

A wildebeest tries to escape a crocodile ambush as it crosses the River Mara in the central African country of Kenya.

CAMOUFLAGE

Many animals blend into their surroundings—branches, rocks, sand, or blossoms—so they will not be seen by other animals. This copying of the background is called **camouflage.** Camouflage is normally associated with defense, as a way to avoid being seen by **predators.** But ambushing predators can use this method as well, making it hard for potential **prey** to notice them until it is too late.

The tawny owl, a native of Asia and Europe, has rusty brown coloring with light and dark patches that look like the rough, partly shaded bark of a tree. The owl perches motionless on tree branches, almost disappearing. It finds mice and other **rodent** prey from great distances away using its sharp eyesight and hearing. Then, it swoops down silently to clutch the prey in its powerful talons.

Coyotes sometimes hunt in packs, like wolves, but they usually find their prey on their own. Their light brown to grayish fur is perfect camouflage for the desert and scrubland **habitats** of the western United States. Blending into the background makes it easier for the coyote to hunt such prey as rabbits, lizards, and snakes.

The coloring of the coyote matches that of its grassland habitat.

A fish-eating insect?

The giant water bug is the largest European water **insect,** growing more than 3 inches (7.5 centimeters) long. As a **larva,** the water bug lurks on freshwater plants, blending in to the plant stalks and fronds. When a small **amphibian, crustacean,** or fish comes near, the bug strikes. It injects strong digestive saliva into the prey and sucks out the insides after they have turned to liquid.

The plumage (feathers) of the tawny owl helps it to blend into its woodland background.

Scavenging

Most **carnivorous** animals will eat the flesh of an animal that they did not kill themselves. Through scavenging instead of hunting, a meat eater both saves energy and avoids the risk of getting hurt. But such chances do not come up often. Animals that scavenge must be ready to eat this food source as soon as they find it.

FREE LUNCH

A **"predator"** sometimes becomes a **"scavenger."** Most predators cannot eat old, rotten remains—they will get sick. But they will eat a fresh **carcass** if they find one. Even such top predators as great white sharks (see page 8) are not above scavenging on the carcass of whales or other large sharks.

Animals cannot count on **carrion** as a food source. Many animals might die suddenly all at once, such as from a flood or disease, or there might be very few deaths during some parts of the year. So even animals that usually scavenge will catch **prey** if they have to. Lammergeiers (*LAM uhr gy uhrz),* also called bearded vultures, are birds that live in the mountains of Africa, Asia, and Europe. They pick up bones in their talons and fly to great heights. Then, they drop the bones onto rocks, breaking them open to expose the soft **tissue** inside. But these smart birds use the same method to kill small animals, such as turtles, when they cannot find enough bones.

Some animals closely related to each other may use different feeding methods. Striped and brown hyenas, for example, are infamous for their scavenging, arriving to eat the leftovers from a lion or cheetah kill. But their relatives, spotted hyenas, are serious predators, hunting down more than half—and possibly as much as 95 percent—of their food.

Scavengers including a spotted hyena, black-backed jackal, vultures, and marabou storks feed on the leftovers of a wildebeest kill in the Maasai Mara National Reserve, Kenya.

City scavengers

Not all scavenging happens in wild **habitats.** Many animals make use of human garbage by searching landfills, garbage cans, and city environments for uneaten food. Foxes and raccoons have a long history of scavenging in cities. Such birds as sea gulls live at landfills, picking through the trash to find scraps.

Sea gulls search for food on a garbage dump.

A CLOSER LOOK

Whale Falls

The dark ocean floor thousands of feet or meters down is a mysterious place, but modern technology has allowed scientists to investigate this world of intense pressures (the weight of the water pressing down) and total darkness. One of the most active, life-supporting **habitats** there is a direct result of death.

Nutrients usually fall to the lower levels of the ocean from shallower waters in the form of waste, uneaten bits of food, or dead things. Much of this type of food is eaten by animals in the middle layers of the ocean. Little is left to sink to the sea floor. But the dead bodies of some ocean-dwelling animals, such as large sharks and whales, are too big to be completely eaten in the upper and middle levels of the ocean. When a whale **carcass** settles onto the seabed, it sets off a unique, slow-motion feeding frenzy that can last for decades.

The high pressure and cold temperature of the water near the seabed slow down the rotting of the whale carcass. For the first few months, **scavengers,** such as ratfish, hagfish, and deep-sea sharks, drawn to the scent of whale flesh, feast on the carcass's soft **tissue.** Then worms, **crustaceans,** and **mollusks** eat the whale's blubber (fat) for up to two years.

Even the whale's skeleton is an important food source to some types of animals. **Bacteria** break down fats inside the bones. The bacteria attract many other ocean-dwelling **species** that eat them, including mussels, snails, and worms. One animal, called the zombie worm, settles on whale bones and grows into them with roots, like a plant. The roots break down the hard part of the bone. The worms then take in the leftover nutritious tissue in the bone through their skin. This material feeds bacteria living in the roots. Zombie worms then digest the bacteria. The bacteria and animals break down the bones slowly, so it can take decades before the entire carcass is completely eaten.

The diverse community of animals travels from far and wide to the sites of these whale falls. Most use very little energy outside of feeding, likely going months or even years between meals.

Six years after the carcass of this GRAY WHALE settled on the seafloor 5,492 feet (1,674 meters) below the surface, the skeleton hosts a whole community of animals that feed off it.

OBLIGATE SCAVENGERS

A few animals must scavenge to survive. They specialize in eating **carrion** and cannot catch their own **prey.** Such animals are called obligate (*OHB luh gayt*) **scavengers.** For example, blowflies must lay their **eggs** on rotting meat, a **carcass,** or the open wound of a living animal. The **larvae** hatch there and eat the flesh.

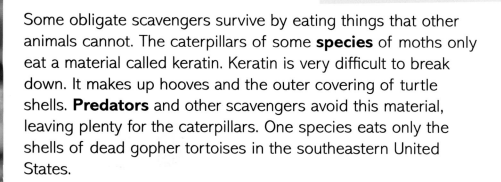

The blowfly lays its eggs on carrion so that the larvae have a food source.

Some obligate scavengers survive by eating things that other animals cannot. The caterpillars of some **species** of moths only eat a material called keratin. Keratin is very difficult to break down. It makes up hooves and the outer covering of turtle shells. **Predators** and other scavengers avoid this material, leaving plenty for the caterpillars. One species eats only the shells of dead gopher tortoises in the southeastern United States.

THE LAST BITS AND PIECES

Some animals are not picky eaters. **Detritivores** are the **omnivores** of the scavenging world, eating whatever they can find. This can be rotting leaves, bits of carrion, or even skin and hair shed from living animals. This stuff is called **detritus.** Like scavengers, detritivores help move **nutrients** through the food web. **Bacteria** break down detritivores' waste and release the nutrients into the soil when they die, allowing them to be taken up again by plants. Millipedes are a common detritivore. They use their dozens of legs to cruise around forest floors looking for fallen leaves and rotting wood to eat.

Roadkill

One of the biggest ways humans have changed the habits and **ranges** of animals is through the building of roads. Each day, drivers kill many millions of animals trying to cross roads. These deaths, called roadkill, are a huge source of food to scavenging animals. Though such accidents have only been happening for about 100 years, some animals now rely on them. For example, hawks may perch above highways and high-traffic roads, waiting for an animal to dart out in front of a car. But while eating roadkill, scavengers run the risk of being hit by cars themselves.

This millipede is eating rotting tree bark.

A CLOSER LOOK

Vultures

When many people hear the word **"scavenger,"** the first animal they think of is a group of birds called vultures. Vultures have many traits that allow them to survive on **carrion** alone. While some of these traits make vultures unpleasant to humans, they also make them very efficient at finding, traveling to, and digesting rotting meat, all while surviving in the hot, dry climates in which they live.

To spot and fly to **carcasses,** vultures fly tens of thousands of feet or thousands of meters into the air, higher than any other bird. The low levels of oxygen so high up would kill other birds. But the cells that make up a vulture's blood can push more oxygen into its body **tissues,** allowing it to fly at these heights. The bird soars and glides on its long, broad wings, going minutes at a time without flapping.

Vultures use their keen senses to find rotting carrion as they circle high above the landscape. Some **species** have sharp eyesight to spot carcasses on open plains. Others have a keen sense of smell. They can track the scent of decay to a carcass, even if it is blocked from view by trees. A few species, such as the turkey vulture of North and South America, have both sharp eyesight and a strong sense of smell.

The heads and necks of many vultures lack feathers. For years, people believed that they were bare to prevent bits of rotting meat (which could cause infection and sickness) from sticking to the bird as it ate. But some **zoologists** now think that this bare flesh allows body heat to escape, helping the bird to cool down on hot days. In colder weather, the bird pulls its long neck close to its body to stay warm.

Vultures also urinate and defecate (*YUR uh nayt, DEHF uh kayt;* get rid of liquid and solid body wastes) on their legs and feet. Like their bare head, this may help keep them cool. When the urine and liquid in the feces (*FEE seez;* solid wastes) evaporates, it carries heat away from the bird's body, just like evaporating sweat.

Vultures use powerful stomach acid to break down their food. The acid kills most harmful **bacteria,** allowing vultures to eat rotten meat without getting sick. If startled or threatened, vultures will simply spit up their stomach contents. This foul-smelling liquid is usually enough to drive attackers away.

VULTURES fight over a carcass in the Kruger National Park, South Africa.

Grazing

Many of the plant-eating animals of the world's huge open plains—such as North America's prairies and the Eurasian steppes—form large herds to graze (eat grasses). These animals must eat a lot of grass and spend a long time digesting it to get enough **nutrients.**

TIME TO DIGEST

Most of the grasses eaten by grazing animals do not contain much energy. The animals need to eat lots of this food and squeeze all the nutrients that they can from it. Digesting plants takes a long time because it contains large amounts of a tough material called cellulose.

Grazing animals have body parts and systems that allow them to digest their tough food. Most of them have large teeth with broad surfaces to grind down grasses. But grazers also have a complex digestive system that allows them to get energy out of such tough food.

FOUR STOMACHS?

Cows, goats, sheep, and many other grazing **species** have four sections in their stomachs to help them digest tough plants. In the first section, called the rumen, **bacteria** start to break down the swallowed plant material. In the second, called the reticulum, the plant material is filtered to remove larger bits. The larger pieces are brought back up to the mouth from the rumen and reticulum. The grazer then chews and swallows them again. For some bits of food, this process can be repeated up to 50 times. The third section, called the omasum, removes water from the mixture. The fourth section, called the abomasum, breaks down the food more before it is sent to the intestines, which finally take in the nutrients.

Bacteria inside you

Almost all animals have large groups of bacteria in their digestive systems. These bacteria are especially important for animals that eat plants, because they help the animals break down cellulose. Other kinds of bacteria may not help digestion, but instead crowd out harmful bacteria. Scientists are just beginning to learn how these bacteria interact with the animal in which they live—including humans. They think that imbalances among groups of bacteria could lead to obesity, illnesses of the digestive system, and even some cancers.

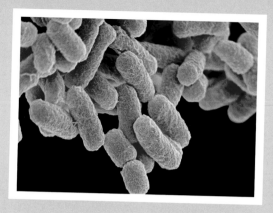

These rod-shaped bacteria are a normal part of the human digestive system.

Cattle graze on dry grassland in northeastern Turkey.

HERD INSTINCT

Grazing animals usually live in open areas where grass is plentiful. North America's Great Plains, the steppes of eastern Europe and northern Asia, and the Serengeti Plain in east Africa are huge, flat expanses of grass.

These grasslands are home to huge groups of grazing animals, which move along as they look for the richest feeding grounds. They often follow a seasonal pattern of cold and warm or wet and dry periods. The large supply of food can support these huge populations.

Grazing animals often feed in huge herds of hundreds or thousands of individuals. They do not need other animals to help them find food, since their **habitats** are usually covered in it. Instead, grazers group together for protection from **predators.** The many eyes and ears of the herd allow predators to be spotted quickly. Individual members may take turns acting as sentries (guardians) ready to tell the herd of approaching danger. Herds of topi antelope in Africa, for example, have sentries to warn of such predators as cheetahs, hunting dogs, lions, and leopards.

Topi antelopes stand guard on a small mound.

South America's guanacos, relatives of camels, live in less grass-rich plains—often near deserts or more than 12,000 feet (3,600 meters) above sea level. Although food is less plentiful, guanacos still gather in herds for defense. If attacked by a mountain lion or a fox, the herd dashes away together. Scientists think that running in a group confuses the predator and makes it harder to target one animal.

Grazing under the sea?

The green sea turtle is the only **herbivore** among the seven **species** of sea turtle. Green sea turtles weigh up to 400 pounds (180 kilograms) and travel long distances between their feeding grounds and the beaches where they lay their **eggs.** Young sea turtles eat **crustaceans, plankton,** and worms. But as they grow, their diet shifts to seagrass, which grows in warm, shallow waters. Green turtles graze in these undersea meadows. Their beaks have jagged edges that help them grasp and tear the slippery seagrass.

A green sea turtle grazes on seagrass.

A herd of guanacos grazes on the high plains of the Torres del Paine National Park, in Patagonia, Chile.

Browsing

Browsing is another way of getting food from plants. But unlike grazing animals, which eat low-lying grasses, browsing animals eat buds, twigs, and leaves higher up from the ground.

PICKY EATERS

Browsing animals look for foods that offer more nutrition than grasses. This means they can eat less food than grazers, and that their digestion process can be simpler. But they must take more time to find the right plants to eat.

Giraffes live on wide open expanses in Africa, such as the Serengeti Plain. They avoid this sea of grass—and the competition from the herds of grazers that would come with it—in favor of the few trees that dot the landscape. The long neck of a giraffe helps it reach more leaves of the acacia (*uh KAY shuh),* mimosa, and wild apricot trees found in its **range.**

DIFFERENT APPROACHES

The difference between grazing and browsing is not always clear-cut. **Zoologists** have even found evidence that animals that normally graze will sometimes switch to browsing. The diet of feral (wild) horses in Australia includes many shrub and tree leaves. It could be that these foods are natural medicines to the animal or simply add **nutrients** to their diets that are not present in grasses.

Some animal **species** are closely related, but behave very differently as they feed. Sheep, for example, are textbook grazers, with flocks spending hours in grassy meadows and fields. Goats are close relatives, but they browse on bushes and branches. Even the two main species of bison are different. North American bison graze the grasses of the Great Plains. But the European bison has adapted to a marshy, wooded environment by browsing to find its food.

Giraffes browse on trees in Buffalo Springs National Park, in Kenya.

Mythical browser

One African browsing animal, the okapi, is so secretive—feeding in thick woodlands and often out of sight—that people once thought it was a mythical creature, like a unicorn. But this striped relative of the giraffe has advantages that help it feed in dense, far-away tropical forests. It can stretch its 16-inch (40-centimeter) black tongue around leaves and buds and yank them from branches.

The okapi uses its long tongue to reach leaves and buds.

OVERBROWSING

Grazers eat quick-growing grasses and grains, so it is hard for them to hurt their environment. On the other hand, browsers often harm and kill trees that take decades to regrow, and eat the young shoots that would replace them. In this way, browsers can completely change an environment if they eat too much.

It is easy to see where moose or caribou (*KAR uh boo*) have been browsing. They strip off the bark of many forest trees, leaving them vulnerable to infection. Fortunately, their small populations, combined with their preference to live in places that are far away from people, allow the woodlands to recover from such browsing.

A moose strips the bark from a tree in Yellowstone National Park in the United States.

Today, the grazing of the white-tailed deer can change **habitats.** Tens of thousands of years ago in North America, deer and other browsers were hunted by bears, mountain lions, and wolves. When humans arrived on the continent, they began to change the environment and hunt many animals. Natural **predators' ranges** were greatly reduced, and many browsers, including the white-tailed deer, were hunted nearly to **extinction.** As the United States and Canada began limiting hunting in the early 1900's, deer populations bounced back. But large predators, facing broken-up ranges and resistance from people, have been slow to return. With reduced human hunting and few natural predators left, some deer populations grew beyond what the environment could hold.

Today, conservationists throughout North America are concerned about overbrowsing by white-tailed deer. The worst-affected areas are the lowest level of forests and woodland. Large sections of the continent's forests show a browse line where tree branches have been cleared to as high as deer can reach and new shoots are eaten as soon as they appear. Ground-nesting birds, snails, and **insects** are threatened by this loss of plants.

A family of white-tailed deer eat rose bushes in a garden in the western U.S. state of California.

International action

Conservation groups and international agreements have looked to reduce the loss of wildlife and harm to habitats. That same cooperation has also led to international studies and projects to deal with overbrowsing. Scientists studied two forested islands off the coast of western Canada. One island had deer, and the other had none. They fenced off parts of the island with deer to create refuges for plants, and compared them to areas from the island that never had deer. The results suggested that plant refuges could help improve the environment of overbrowsed areas.

Filter Feeding

In ponds, lakes, and oceans, food can drift through the water in what look like clouds. Some animals can gulp up such food with the water around it. Once their **prey** is in their mouth, they spit out the water and swallow the prey. This efficient feeding behavior is called filter feeding.

CLOUDS OF FOOD

Many fish, sharks, and whales cruise the oceans, mouths open, letting their food flow in. The huge whale shark is the largest fish in the world, reaching a length of at least 40 feet (12 meters). It grows to its large size through filter feeding. Special pads in the shark's mouth filter **plankton** as water passes through the gills. The flow of the water pushes the lump of plankton to the back of the mouth, where it can be swallowed.

BIRDS

Although most filter feeders are ocean-dwelling animals, some **species** of birds filter food out of estuaries, marshes, and ponds. (An estuary [*EHS chu EHR ee*] is the wide mouth of a river into which ocean tides flow.) Flamingos use hairlike "combs" along the edges of the bill to strain tiny animals from mud and sand. Some species of ducks have tiny, comb-like shapes called lamellae, which they use to trap tiny animals and seeds from mouthfuls of silt or water.

A huge whale shark opens its mouth to collect tiny plankton.

STAYING IN PLACE

If an animal cannot move, filter feeding is the best way for it to gather food. Sponges are some of the simplest animals, but they use filter feeding to survive in ocean **habitats** all over the world. Water enters sponges through small pores called ostia. In these pores, special cells filter bits of food from the water. The filtered water, along with any wastes, passes into the large, chimney-like osculum, from where it leaves the sponge. Other filter feeding animals that cannot move (or do not move much) include some corals, shellfish, and barnacles (*BAHR nuh kuhlz*).

The barrel sponge is a filter feeder.

Humpback Whales

The giant humpback whale has some of the most complex feeding habits of any filter feeder. It does some amazing things to catch hundreds or thousands of **prey** at one time.

Like other filter-feeding whales, a humpback has long plates of baleen (*buh LEEN)* hanging from its upper jaw. These baleen plates are full of bristles, allowing water to pass through them, but stopping small animals from escaping. A whale opens its huge mouth to take in thousands of gallons or liters of water. It then closes its mouth, allowing the water to flow out through its baleen. When the water is gone, the whale swallows the animals left behind.

Humpbacks eat different kinds of prey, including shrimplike **crustaceans** called krill, squid, and small fish. Humpbacks' long pectoral flippers make them more agile than other baleen whales. They are one of the only baleen whale **species** known to work in teams. They often form groups of 10 or more for hunting and feeding.

One hunting method used by the whales is bubble-net feeding. Several humpbacks surround a group of prey. One or more of the whales dives lower and blows bubbles from its blowhole (the breathing hole on its head) while swimming in a circle below the prey. The prey will not swim through the bubbles, so become trapped inside the circle. The whales then take turns swimming through the bubble net to gather mouthfuls of prey.

The whales also use a method called lunge-feeding. After finding and corralling a group of prey, the whale dives up at it from below. The humpback swims up through the mass of prey with its mouth open, breaking through the surface of the water (called breaching). Sometimes, lunge-feeding whales cooperate to better control larger masses of prey.

Humpback whales use many different variations of the bubble net and lunge-feeding methods. These behaviors are learned, not instinctual—or something a whale is born knowing how to do. A young humpback watches how its mother and other adults in its group corral prey and copies them. In this way, the feeding styles of humpbacks vary from place to place.

HUMPBACK WHALES lunge feed in Monterey Bay, near the coast of California.

Finding Food Year-Round

Most animals must be able to find food year-round. As the seasons change, more or less food may be present. Different kinds of animals deal with seasonal changes in food supply in different ways.

MIGRATION

As conditions change, some animals travel to different places to find food. Such seasonal travel is called migration. Though migration takes energy, the animals that migrate are rewarded with more chances to feed and more stable conditions. Many **species** of birds are famous for their long migrations, with some traveling thousands of miles or kilometers each year.

Some of the most dramatic movements of animals are across Africa's Serengeti plain after the rainy season has begun. Dry, withered grasses turn green again, attracting millions of grazing animals and **predators** wanting to hunt them. The animals crossing the Serengeti form the largest **mammal** migration in the world. The fresh grass attracts 750,000 zebras, 1.2 million wildebeests, and hundreds of thousands of other plains animals.

In colder areas, many grazing animals travel long distances southward as winter approaches, and back north as fresh grass grows in the spring. The movement of reindeer across Siberia, a huge area in northern Asia, is a dramatic example.

The search for food is also common in the oceans. Southern right whales spend four months eating **plankton** near Antarctica before traveling about 1,500 miles (2,400 kilometers) to breed (make more animals like themselves) near South Africa, South America, and Australia. They do not feed until they return to Antarctica—eight months later.

Wildebeests and zebras prepare to cross a river during the great migration across the Serengeti, in southern Africa.

PREPARATION

Other animals stay in one place, but prepare for the leaner months. Animals as small as dormice and bats and as large as bears get ready for colder weather by eating a great deal in the autumn. They build up body fat, which acts as a blanket and energy source as they **hibernate** over the winter. Squirrels, on the other hand, cannot pack on body fat so easily and do not hibernate. They also spend the autumn in search of acorns and nuts, but they do not eat them right away. Instead, they bury this food or store it in hollows of trees. They eat these hidden reserves when food is scarce in the winter months. Chipmunks hibernate, but wake briefly every few days. If their fat reserves are running low, they can also eat food that they have stored.

ADAPTATION

Species of animals have also changed over millions of years to find food where they live, even if that is hard to do during some parts of the year. The wide hoof of a musk ox can be used as a shovel to dig through a snowfall in search of grass below. In northern Alaska, flat bark beetles have a special chemical mix in their blood that acts as antifreeze. It allows them to hunt smaller **insects** under tree bark in temperatures as low as -70 °F (-56 °C).

The musk ox can find food in the snowy conditions of an Arctic winter.

This chipmunk has stuffed its cheeks with food. It will carry it back to its nest and store it for the winter.

Life in Death Valley?

California's Death Valley receives just 2 inches (5 centimeters) of rain each year. The valley is home to many kinds of animals, all of which can survive the heat and find food and water, sometimes in strange ways. Kangaroo rats never need to drink water: they get their moisture from their diet of grass seeds and mesquite beans. Jackrabbits use their huge ears to give off heat as they browse low shrubs. Roadrunners, fast-running birds, have a naturally high body temperature (about 104 °F or 40 °C) so they can hunt for insects and small **rodents** in the midday heat. A number of larger **predators** patrol Death Valley as well, including coyotes, foxes, bobcats, and mountain lions.

This roadrunner has caught a worm, but roadrunners also hunt larger prey, including lizards and rattlesnakes.

Habitat Change

Natural conditions can change, sometimes gradually (for example, a drought that lasts a long time) or overnight (after a flash flood or blizzard). The change may last for a short time, such as unusual weather, or a long time, such as **climate change** or **habitat** destruction. Animals must adjust to food shortages that are caused by these events. The adjustments may be fairly simple, such as looking harder and longer for food, or they may involve big changes in the way the animal finds food.

NATURAL DISASTERS

Natural disasters, such as wildfires, floods, tornadoes, and hurricanes, can destroy an animal's food supply in a matter of hours. Some animals rely on their own body adaptations to keep them alive when food becomes scarce. Camels' humps, for example, are full of fat that can give them energy.

Other animals change their feeding method to deal with a changed habitat. The spotted hyena turns easily from hunting to scavenging when drought or bad weather strikes. If food becomes scarce because of a natural disaster, some **species** of birds irrupt. An irruption is an irregular movement to a different area. Although the birds will have to compete for food with animals already in the new area, their chances for survival are better than they would be in their home **range.**

A camel stores fat in its hump, which it can use for energy when there is no food.

Taking advantage

Some animals make use of natural disasters to find food. Mountain lions, bears, and other **predators** often patrol the edge of forest fires, waiting to pounce on animals running from the flames. After natural disasters, meat-eating animals may return to eat the **carcasses** of the animals that did not survive. For example, woodpeckers arrive in charred forests to eat bark beetles that have died in forest fires.

A mountain lion on the lookout for prey. Mountain lions sometimes find food after forest fires.

CHANGES MADE BY HUMANS

Today, humans are one of the most powerful forces of change on the planet. Animals that cannot adapt to these changes die, but some can even make use of changes brought on by humans. Eurasian blackcaps are birds that spend their summers in central and Eastern Europe. Today, some individuals migrate to Great Britain and Ireland in the winter, rather than to Spain and Portugal as the rest of the birds do. More people in Great Britain and Ireland put out bird feeders than do people in Portugal and Spain. The birds endure a harsher winter, but have a shorter migration distance and a large, easy-to-find food supply.

INVASIVE SPECIES

With human-caused environmental changes, some **species** can spread out of control, destroying other plants and animals. Such animals are called **invasive species.** Black and brown rats were originally from Asia, but they stowed away on the ships of European traders and are now found throughout the world. Their ability to eat almost any food allowed them to spread. Such rats probably ate grains, seeds, and **detritus** before people started living in large groups, but now they mostly eat leftovers from humans. When they were introduced to new areas, they often wiped out many local animals by eating their food or raiding their nests. Nest raiding was especially harmful for birds on ocean islands. When humans arrived on an island, rats hidden on their ships would escape and drive most of the native bird species to **extinction** in a few years.

Although a few kinds of animals have found success living alongside humans, most struggle just to survive. They may become sick, and their populations may be reduced to a fraction of their normal size. Some may learn to live on human scraps or at landfills, but such diets are usually unhealthy for them.

Shoebill

One of Africa's most distinctive and mysterious birds is the shoebill. Shoebills live in marshes and swamps in eastern Africa, normally standing very still and ambushing fish. But shoebill populations are declining because of hunting and destruction of their **habitat.** International conservation groups list the shoebill as "vulnerable." With their natural food supply reduced, shoebills have turned to scavenging, eating scraps left over from lions and other African **predators.**

The shoebill gets its name from its huge bill, which looks like a wooden shoe.

A blackcap perches on a bird feeder in a U.K. garden.

FINDING A BALANCE

For thousands of years, human beings have been changing the environment, forcing **species** to adapt or go **extinct.** Hunting, fishing, land use practices, pollution, and now **climate change** have affected how animals find food. Some species have adapted, but many more—possibly millions—have gone extinct.

Humans can learn from our past mistakes and try to leave environments where native animals can find food and survive. In the 1800's, overhunting nearly drove the North American bison to extinction. Action from the U.S. federal government, including the creation of a national park system, allowed herds of wild bison to survive on protected lands in their native prairie **habitat.**

The European bison was not so lucky. Its last wild populations—in Eastern Europe and by the Caucasus Mountains—were gone by the 1920's. But breeding programs in zoos kept the species from extinction. European conservationists followed the United States' example in creating natural reserves where the bison were reintroduced.

A baby green sea turtle makes its way to the ocean after hatching. Sea turtle nesting sites are threatened by climate change.

Welcome home?

More than 200 sheep fell to their deaths in southern France in July 2017. A brown bear chased them off a cliff. The last wild bear had been killed in that part of France in 2004. Since then, conservationists have reintroduced bears to their previous hunting grounds, but local farmers are outraged.

Disagreements like this flared up when another **predator**—the wolf—was reintroduced to Yellowstone National Park in the 1990's. Elk herds had grown too large, it was argued, and wolves helped to control the elk population boom. But local ranchers feared that their herds of cattle would become victims of this returning predator.

A brown bear in southern France. Such large predators are often not popular with farmers.

North American bison grazing in Grand Teton National Park. These animals came close to extinction in the 1800's.

Glossary

amphibian a vertebrate with scaleless skin that usually lives part of its life in water and part on land. Vertebrate animals have a backbone.

bacterium (plural bacteria) a single-celled living thing. Some bacteria can cause disease.

camouflage the natural coloring or form of an animal that enables it to blend into its surroundings, making it difficult to see.

carcass the dead body of an animal.

carnivore a meat-eating animal.

carrion the flesh of a dead animal.

climate change a change in the usual weather of a particular place, often associated with global warming.

crustacean a group of mainly aquatic arthropods that includes crabs, lobsters, shrimps, and barnacles. An arthropod is an animal with jointed legs and no backbone.

detritivore an animal that eats bits of discarded organic matter.

detritus any collection of nonliving organic material.

egg a female sex cell, or the structure in which the embryo develops, usually outside the mother's body.

extinct, extinction when every member of a species (kind) of living thing has died.

fungus (plural fungi) a living thing that usually grows on plants or on decaying matter. Yeast and mushrooms are fungi.

habitat the place where a living thing usually makes its home.

herbivore a plant-eating animal.

hibernate to spend the winter in a state like deep sleep. Breathing, heart rate, and other body processes slow down.

insect one of the major invertebrate groups. Invertebrate animals do not have a backbone. Insects have six legs and a three-part body.

invasive species a type of living thing that spreads rapidly in a new environment where there are few or no natural controls on its growth.

larva (plural larvae) the active, immature stage of some animals, such as many insects, that is different from its adult form.

mammal one of the major vertebrate animal groups. Vertebrate animals have a backbone. Mammals feed their offspring on milk produced by the mother, and most have hair or fur.

mollusk a group of invertebrates that includes slugs, snails, mussels, and octopuses. Invertebrate animals do not have a backbone.

nutrient a substance that is needed to keep a living thing alive and help it grow.

omnivore an animal that eats plants and animals.

plankton tiny living things that drift at or near the surface of oceans, lakes, and other bodies of water.

predator an animal that hunts, kills, and eats other animals.

prey an animal that is hunted, killed, and eaten by another.

range the area in which a species can be found.

reptile one of the major vertebrate animal groups. Vertebrate animals have a backbone. A reptile has dry, scaly skin and breathes air. Snakes, crocodiles, and lizards are all reptiles.

rodent a mammal with front teeth made for gnawing hard things.

scavenger an animal that feeds on the carcasses of dead animals.

shoal a group of fish.

species a group of living things that have certain permanent traits in common and are able to reproduce (make more living things like themselves) with each other.

tissue the material of which living things are made.

venom a naturally produced liquid that animals can introduce into other animals (for example, through biting) in order to stun, injure, or kill the other animal.

venomous describes an animal that produces venom or a part of such an animal that releases venom.

warm-blooded describes an animal that is able to control its body temperature.

zoologist a scientist who studies animals.

BOOKS

Adapted to Survive: Animals That Hunt by Angela Royston (Raintree Books, 2014)

Coral Reef Food Chains (Who Eats What?) by Rebecca Pettiford (Pogo Books, 2016)

DK Ocean: A Visual Encylopedia (DK Children, 2015)

Life and the Flow of Energy by William B. Rice (Teacher Created Materials, 2015)

WEBSITES

African Wildlife Foundation
http://www.awf.org/
Organization that works to protect the unique wildlife of Africa.

RSPB Birds and Wildlife Food Chains
https://www.rspb.org.uk/birds-and-wildlife/read
-and-learn/fun-facts-and-articles/foodchains
/findingfood.aspx
Check out this article from the Royal Society for the Protection of Birds on how birds find food.

Serengeti National Park
http://www.serengeti.org/
The official website of Serengeti National Park in Tanzania.

Smithsonian Magazine—Animals and Humans Finding Food
https://www.smithsonianmag.com/smart-news
/animals-and-humans-use-similar-tactics-to-find
-food-180948199/
Human hunter-gatherer groups search for food using the same method many animals do.

Index